The Green of Ordinary Time

The Green of Ordinary Time

Laura Fargas

Washington Writers' Publishing House
Washington, D.C.

Copyright © 2016 by Laura Fargas
All rights reserved

COVER PAINTING "Green Wheat Fields, Auvers" by Vincent Van Gogh
COVER DESIGN by Barbara Shaw
TYPESETTING by Barbara Shaw

LIBRARY OF CONGRESS CATALOGUING-IN-PUBLICATION DATA
Names: Fargas, Laura, author
Title: The green of ordinary time / Laura Fargas.
Description: Washington, D.C. : Washington Writers' Publishing House, [2016]
  | Includes bibliographical references.
Identifiers: LCCN 2016042075 | ISBN 9781941551127 (pbk : alk. paper)
Classification: LCC PS3556.A7138 A6 2016 | DDC 811/.54--dc23
LC record available at https://lccn.loc.gov/2016042075

Printed in the United States of America
WASHINGTON WRITERS' PUBLISHING HOUSE
P. O. Box 15271
Washington, D.C. 20003

for my mother,
Marilyn Anderson Thompson

Contents

I

3 Limbo, That Abolished World
4 Survival of the Good Enough
5 Alas
6 St. Praxeda Sopping Up Blood (Vermeer)
7 *Godspell*
8 Of All Earthly Things
9 Cézanne
10 Apple
11 Woman Holding Balance (Vermeer)
12 Friday
13 Wishbone
14 Liam
15 But Never a Smile Without a Cat
16 Third Snow in a Week
17 No Other
18 Dain Bramage, Private Eye on the Case
19 *Vieux Port*
20 Rain You Are Not
21 Poplar Pond, November
22 August

23 *Suite: Little Compton*
24 Fog Day
25 Sun Day
26 The Lady on the Beach
27 Flotation
28 Millennium

II

31 There is No Murder
32 For Laura C.
33 Everything AND the Circus
34 For the Homely Protestant (Robert Motherwell)
35 On the Way in this Morning
36 Doggederel
37 Mississippi John Hurt
38 A House of Three Animals
39 To Bach
40 "…Posing as a Somdomite"
41 Wanting the Answer
42 Mourning, Saturday
43 Hymn to Apollo (*Phaedo* para. 29)
44 A Dish Best Eaten Cold
45 Chopin at Nohant
46 Darkness Travels at the Speed of Light
47 Lust
48 Old Flames
49 The Same Apple Twice
50 The High Romantics Confront Mont Blanc
51 George Gorging, Lord B.
52 The Victorian Age
53 That Photo of Jack & Jerry
54 The Marriage
55 First Love
56 Save Time
57 Raskolnikov
58 Heirs
59 Aubade
60 Lifework

63	Suite: *Riverside, Iowa (Stumptown)*
64	Some Kind of Prayer
66	So Far
67	After Midnight
68	The Change I Was Afraid of & Wanted
69	Closer
70	Notes
73	Acknowledgments
75	About the Author

I

Limbo, That Abolished World

For five seconds or so, backwards seems possible,
the heirloom un-be-smithereenable. When the voice
first said, gently, "We lost her," Wally roared,
"Then go find her!"
Freeze frame: this is Simon and me at the pier,
alive in some previous hour.
Happy, we were happy beyond disbelief.

Survival of the Good Enough

It isn't the fittest. It's the pelican
dropping like a stone toward the fish while
all around her seagulls do the same work elegantly.
Or me at night, with twenty/two thousand vision,
touching my way to the fridge, finding orange juice,
sweet and sharply cold. She and I all but safe in our niches
unless the finch with a better beak comes along.

Alas!

Because the other language hides in my mind
all the time, each cry, each suspirant
despair, has needed translation. And so failed.
"Alas," she cries, "alas, all is lost,
all are dead." *Wings*, says my inner ear,
Wings! All are lost and dead, wings, wings!
Where shall I go, what shall I do, wings, wings?

St. Praxeda Sopping Up Blood (Vermeer)

How beautiful he lets the blood be,
Christian river hitting the pagan ground,
marble tiles where the saint can take off her apron,
press it, and transfer red from white to linen.
Why this story? This little pity for the dead? I did it once,
sopped up my neighbor's blood after the ambulance left,
but it was the living I had in mind, his wife.

Godspell

I got the tango with Jesus. The spotlight
hits and I slut down the aisle, singing
"Turn Back, O Man, Deny Thy Foolish Ways."
His lines in scribbles all over the scaffolding –
Jesus has these really long monologues – I sling
my feather boa, he dips me – "for life is
– *something* – and none may count their days."

Of All Earthly Things

High summer dream and drowse. Waves
scrape the littoral, drain back to sea. Heat
pure as light. Pale morning hours,
trees like priests wearing the green of ordinary time.
Fruits dizzy with their juices. Leaves
at full flesh. Of all earthly things, Paradise
was most like this.

Cézanne

is right, the pear is always
askew at the brink, always in danger of falling
straight out of the world of sphere
toward the floor we don't often see, that might be
painted a rosy brown or gray-green and still tilt
into the landscape that needs brushstrokes
to complete it, to fill in – but he doesn't always – the blanks.

Apple

Of my eye. Of greeny temptation,
lake of the skin, glacier within. Strange places
it took us, wandering, discovering thorns and
beasts who shied away from us. Making words
that weren't names for all the complicated
things we now needed to say. Heart's red,
lump-footed fruit, sweet, tart, gate out of paradise.

Woman Holding Balance (Vermeer)

Gold and pearls in their raw state as wealth.
She weighs them as she will be weighed,
for pure fineness. Behind her hangs a vision of Christ
sifting the blessed from the damned.
She is close to childbed but seems unafraid,
though the swelling of her dress, poking past her jacket
crescent as a moon, bears the painting's only red.

Friday

Thursday, when was that?
(Oriented times one, oriented times two.)
Feet want the green grass so much.
Chickadee song contest, topping each other,
sostenato, forte, fortissimo. The females listening,
choosing. The mockingbird listening,
storing it all away for later, like me.

Wishbone

Once I gave the future a lock of my hair,
looked into its black eyes and asked it to bless me
for nothing. To suffer the shock
of touching me kindly. There was the merest resistance,
a barely-more-than-transparency, then I slipped through.
Into questions, an accretion of answers.
Deer trail turns to footpath, wagon track, interstate.

Liam

You want the thing to be simple as a fish
and instead it is as hard as catching fish.
It will not settle down, its wild neon eye
never shows you anything but surface.
There is depth, but we do not get to see it.
We are forced to belief. To standing in the river
hip deep, casting a nearly invisible line.

But Never a Smile Without a Cat

Hi-ho, hi-ho, it's off to work: past the tall orange amaryllis,
past sparrows feeding their young in the star magnolia.
Hearing them subliminally, maybe; an everyday knowing there are birds,
but not attentive. If we are dull to the world,
might it not dull to us? Like an unvenerated elder who quits
bothering to enunciate; the three hundred identifiable reds
shrugging, slipping to a hundred fifty.

Third Snow in a Week

Yesterday at St. Sulpice and St. Paul-ouest,
two lovers stopped at the corner
and slowly, carefully, leaned into
a kiss, as if two huge clumsy humans
managing to match their lips each to each
was a delicate, dangerous process,
probably best left to experts. But they
were going to try. He held her head
with both hands, lightly, as adults
hold their fingers out to catch a soap
bubble, and just for guidance, as if
he were Mir and she the food from Earth.
Close, closer, a delicate dance in
weightless space, neither quite complete
without the other, yet risking
death if the joining were inexact, he leaned
toward her for long seconds, and she
opened her eyes wide as it happened.

No Other

I want a slinky, sticky lover,
the slither that is seals in the water,
braided mating snakes. I want a hot unconsciousness
tongue hair sweat textured, hurricane tide, angel rage.
Sexual adults making sexual love,
those bouquets, that joy – lost days.

Dain Bramage, Private Eye on the Case

House-proud inside a depression,
abed all day, can't dress, can't even
bask in a murder. What detective
has to suck down 60 mil of Prozac
before catching the crook? But in books,
locked rooms have to surrender their
secrets, so here's mine: I'll live.

Vieux Port

Moping and stale in a holiday city.
Wanting to join the game of speaking French.
A little poem, child-simple. Reading
your first book – my god, is it possible
to be that young? Writing your first book, the same.
Love – what is it, if we use that word
for what we are at twenty, and what at fifty?

Rain You Are Not

Rain you are not modern you
sizzle on my forearm and caress
my eyes you are the voice distilling
spirits in my ear you are a truer
face for time than any clock I wish
everything more deeply inside you

Poplar Pond, November

One of the old ones has fallen in.
The pond has autumn's clarity and layering,
leaves afloat and sunken,
reflections over the bottom's pebbles and scree.
I make up names for the colors of this leaf –
allol, draeth, breen –
while an ant walks all the way up its stem.

August

Currying the donkey, and the dust off his back
makes the day even hotter. But he likes it
and twitches his ears comfortably. Pastoral.
Lucky to do this on a week day, work day,
in busy America, and so on. Somewhere nearby, even
rich people are unhappy. *Lucky.* I say it out loud,
another bit of noise in the day's machinery.

Suite: Little Compton

i

Fog Day

Over there past the wire and orange flags
lie the fragile nests of piping plovers, whose voices
you cannot mistake for any other birds'. A wave comes in,
breaks itself against the land and breaks the land.
Sea wrack, light green, pink. A woman might let herself
believe all her life that the ocean will not
kill her. The cloud lowers its belly down to the sand.
Say the big water is my mother, impassive as the sea.
You will find me at the brink, gripped in the belief
something underneath loves me. This is the world
Whistler thinned his oils nearly to transparency in order
to paint. It needed great care to set the horizontals
so colors would not bleed downward and destroy the picture.

ii

Sun Day

I look through lenses as if I will see
fifteen-times-wave or fifteen-times-green.
Even for binoculars, the wave inside the water is invisible,
green a pleasing accident. From the rock, cormorants
fly off in opposite directions, though one stays,
still holding his wings out to dry. He looks like a kind of Christ
pinned to the seashore, and is not. He will not pit his life
against my sins. The first mottled rock is beautiful,
and the second, but after that it is the excitement of finding
I am looking for. In junior high, we kissed our hands,
practicing to be someone else who loved us.

iii

The Lady on the Beach

She lifts my tail to sex me. I am female
like her, she thinks. I am headless.
There is a strange flat flower where my strong neck was,
white-rimmed, pulpy red and brown shapes,
and delicate white at the center, the spine stump.
She thinks her mind can swallow me. The shark
swallowed as much of me as it wanted
and left the rest to the sea. The tide pushed me here.
It is just another place to rot. She wants
to enter my body and swim. She likes its dead details,
the few nails left, the tiny bone of my finned foot.
She splays the webbing, sorry I am not alive, then
smells her hand and rubs it hard with sand, stones,
kelp, and rinses it off.

iv

Flotation

The sea took the headless seal back for one night
then dropped her on land again that afternoon.
She came to look like a sausage, a red bloat
picked at by gulls. The pretty white ring of fat
that kept her buoyant and warm in the sea
shriveled to gray slime. Later, the others
walked by the dead thing and told me they had tried
to see with my eyes. I had called her a flower,
so they looked for that. Even the man
who came home from the beach with a glowing new tan
and purple beads around his neck was fooled.
It was a way to get something I wanted, having them
come behind my eyes where I have no face.
It is like saying, hey, a blimp, and everyone
looking up. You could use that time
to steal their wallets. This is a longer invisibility,
time enough for a kind of murder. But desire
is not easily fooled. That same day, I handed my camera
to his friend. Now there is a photograph
of Jack and me in which my face and body appall me.
I will not destroy the negative. I saw her
in the hour when she was fresh from the sea, her body
still sweet, and I wanted to swim away in it.

v

Millennium

She tells him to go outside and swing the wet lettuce
a few times around his head. He says he only wants
one potato tonight. She cuts the tomatoes and
the cucumber. They are both thinking of yesterday,
when they feasted on peanut chicken sliced
with fresh melon that had come home with them
from Little Compton. The upstairs neighbor
comes down to shout for a while, though it is not them
he is angry at. She gets on the telephone
with a friend and they talk about how the bakery
got sold and is now a place to buy cheap postcards.
The man comes in with the lettuce mostly dry,
and she tears it up. She has him try the salad,
and they start talking about how someone wants them
to write an article about the millennium,
with remarks from the friend on the phone relayed.
It's time to eat, whispers the man, trying not
to be rude, but hungry. He has done the work
of fending off the neighbor's rant, while she stayed
behind the kitchen door and mixed a dressing.
Taste it, she tells him, and begins to say goodbye.

II

There is No Murder

There is no murder in this slug. Only 'eat.'
The story of this slug is getting from here to there
without 'here' and 'there.' No 'get on the twig, she's leaving.'
The mind trying to conceive its own blindness.
How to live without knowing 'I want to live.'
Find your own kind of food. Listen to the wind for enemies.
Make sure nothing eats the offspring.

For Laura C.

Little girl, they tell me your heart murmurs.
Hearts will do that, no matter how we instruct them.
It takes almost nothing, a shred of flower, a cousin
humming in the next room, and they're off.
Whisper back, sweetheart. Tell your heart you love
its singular melodies. That you'll be the maid
in the mer-mer-mer of its sea.

Everything AND the Circus

Tempting to take it one small good thing at a time,
ravel one thread until fray is fringe.
But what of an afternoon with eleven elephants and
acrobats and plumed white horses and clowns leapfrogging
clowns all down Constitution Avenue? And a brass band
so disrespectfully loud that this is the NOW
when either you go outside or forever you won't?

For the Homely Protestant (Robert Motherwell)

This is dumb, but I wanted to meet you.
I wanted to thank you for the blue motions on paper
and the great flesh of the Elegies.
I wanted to hear the vulgar details and the sublime ones
of the time you died and came back.
I wanted to know how 'Reconciliation' felt underfoot
before you stood it up and trusted it to eyes.

On the Way in this Morning

Two robin's eggs. Hatched, not eaten,
but no cries overhead. Mentally rehearsing
delicate fingerings of the Fantasie-Impromptu. –
"Chopin (I think he can read hearts)"
wrote an enchanted student. "And his rubato
makes even composers miscount time." –
Six weeks from now, beginning to fly.

Doggederel

Suffering through an alley-neighbor's
single combat with a sax, I remind myself
musicians are kindly persons who neither
leave non-biodegradable byproducts
in our rivers nor cut crooked deals
with dictators. They improve my life.
Improve, improve, improve.

Mississippi John Hurt

"I'm satisfied, tickled too, old
enough to marry you…" I fell as far as
there was for me to go into his fathomless eyes,
his mouth like a harp bringing tunes
out of Delta blackness that rattled
my nine year old Los Angeles bones.
I wanted to deserve him.

A House of Three Animals

Each with its own habits. Two that can roam,
one stuck behind fences. One
that gets food for them all. One that snores.
Two that care about ritual. Two
fastidious. All three incapable of offspring.
Rubbing against each other sometimes.
All three sprouting gray hairs and running less.

To Bach

I was cast away & Brandenburg 4
saved my life. Let me lap at its delicate body
mild as a Christ. Cooled the fevery sea.
Would not lie with me but oh how my belly
healed wherever it brushed by.
Tested: why is *why* and why is *as if*?
Why is *is* not enough? And vanished.

"... Posing as a Somdomite"

Mightn't Oscar have magnificently said,
"you pishing marchionette of narrow beds, it is one
good thing to be a sodomite (as indeed your son
and I have been) but another, even finer, thing to pose?
For you have, don't you realize,
the world's most practiced poseur before your eyes."
But Bosie and the wallpaper staid and he fled.

Wanting the Answer

Enlarging feels like the answer, but it is diminution.
Not even playing mentally with the paradox, but
actual looking. Smaller. Smaller. The pebble,
the wrinkle in the pebble's surface, the moth eggs
round and clumped, mimicking dirt but edible,
healing even. And the other nourishment, soul saving.
Hard as it is to stay alive today, staying alive.

Mourning, Saturday

Permeability. Almost not being there.
Wind across the tidepools, almost straight
through me. Some fish rotting, salt spray.
As little of me as possible, hour after hour.
Quiet. And at night in bed, quiet.
Then jabs of pain: you are. Are a body.
Body, like its joys, subject to defect.

Hymn to Apollo (*Phaedo* para. 29)

Socrates in chains, and the little sound,
'a certain voice,' scruple visiting his dreams, says
make music, so he starts to write a small song
for the god whose festival-ship's voyage
has delayed his execution. But it has a fair wind to Delos,
fair wind back, and he has not finished
by the setting of the sun, when the cup comes.

A Dish Best Eaten Cold

After the folktale, the wolf was bitter.
Slunk elegantly to a rock and cooed to the moon.
They know nothing of blue, of tooth,
yet dared to boil me. Said his lover.
I'll fix 'em for you,
I'll shine in a spectrum they can't see.
Every night I'll be their sorrow,
every night they'll mistake me for their joy.

Chopin at Nohant

You might as well fall in love with the sun
as with some men,
and you are equally powerless not to love them.
They will dapple your longing forever.
They will be Chopin at Nohant, playing so that
out on the lawn the girl Solange will hear.
Close at hand stands a portrait, framed in heavy silver,
of the pallid fiancée who elected not to have him.
He kept it by him like a shrine all the while he lived
in his lover's house, charming her children by other men,
dying more slowly under her care.

Darkness Travels at the Speed of Light

We applaud the sun for going under. Gray, grayer,
nightlike, but not quite. All birds silent,
and most insects. Coronal luminescence
holding light's place, a stand in, a ghost lamp,
odd as colors remembered from a dream. The first return
of sunshine, the "diamond ring." Its promise
stronger than most American marriages.

Lust

It's not some turbulence you never heard of before,
it's that same calamity in the veins:
every morsel of your flesh flushing just to be near
him. Him. Every one of his freckles
he won't let you touch. Nor even wash
dust from the road off his feet, like a Biblical host.
The word clicks like knitting needles, *unrequited.*

Old Flames

Loving me's a tough gig, and I gotta love
the guys who did. It's hard, though –
loving the ones who love you. Then hard to keep it up.
Which jumps me to a weary Nolan Ryan
unhappily giving the ball up to a reliever in the ninth.
There's something about finishing. Going
the distance. The difference from winning.

The Same Apple Twice

I keep remembering how he said
you couldn't bite into one without staining the meat.
Egret ice lily egg bone-china white,
only wounded, streaked by the skin's rich red.
Heraclitus, Heisenberg, a boy up a tree on a farm.
And how they proved uncommercial. *No good for butter,
No good for pies. You had to eat them.*

The High Romantics Confront Mont Blanc

"Is there anything as dull as a mountain?"
yawns George Sand. She writes to her lover
Marcel in Marseilles, "I kiss Liszt
chastely twice a day." Dazzled by the Sea of Ice,
Liszt calls Sand unrhapsodic. She shrugs
and rolls a cheroot. But to Marcel she writes,
"my knees were shaking with lust."

George Gorging, Lord B.

And incidentally, Byron at the banquet pouring
vinegar on his spuds, how high-romantical is that?
Mad, bad, and dangerous to feed, poor lad,
slurping ale from a skull and repenting
nothing so much as extra calories. Ah, Don Juan,
here's something to chew on: if you pulled that shit
now, you could be a bestseller all over again.

The Victorian Age

"I had not thought she would look
so much like an old apple woman," sniffed a peer
meeting his cozy dumpling of a Queen.
Wrapped in black for sixty years. Possessed unto death
of every scrap of undergarment she'd ever had.
High in Windsor, she scribbled in her tiny hand
how disappointing Bertie remained.

That Photo of Jack & Jerry

They were yearling stallions together
and galloped the streets of Paris and drank
the worst wines gladly and haunted the bookstalls.
What a myth, what a fact. My tent is
staked in bankbooks, and it took a pigeon
hatching into his nest of shit and broomstraws
to show me how hard it is to be born.

The Marriage

One morning they fucked delicately,
cool and passionate as a minuet, a ritual
bridging beast-mating and civilization,
room in it for an elegant crooking of their knees
and deeply groaned come-cries, sex with a slight
film of sweat like a dew that rises in a garden
where someone has come to sketch.

First Love

I loved twice and both were cheats.
I loved thrice and all were alcoholics.
I loved four times and each man is balding now.
I started once to love a boy whose father
was very famous, whispering, "I can't believe
I can have what I want." And I couldn't.
And it's rude to start every sentence with "I."

Save Time

You can't. I can't. Kant can't. It's damned, lost,
shot to hell, burned beyond recognition, song gone,
bell tolled, bloom never refurled but shriveled and dust,
cursed, crossed, more sinned against than sinning,
winning, pining, Augustine on his knees screaming
tempus tempus, tempest, tempt us, cant,
can't, you can't, savior, save. You. In time.

Raskolnikov

As if the angels eroded. No longer
clotted the air. As if either mundane happiness or shame
were a fabric brittle from hanging in the light.
As if thought were a solitary act.
So, then, water might lift her dark body from mud,
the moon shy away from our foreplay.

Heirs

Already they were spoiling it. Using the best
crystal for ordinary kitchen drinking,
pretending they were what he really had been,
splendid. You don't want to say they were maggots
but they were breaking the body down. It made
the bones more visible that much earlier.
Necessary so the world can go on, but miserably ugly.

Aubade

While my friend was dying, we enjoyed
singing to each other in the dark
the way we would have, we agreed,
if we'd been lovers. The torchier,
the better. This morning in the maples
there's a warbler whose song I've known before
only from mockingbirds.

Lifework

What hard work it is to be the living.
How much easier they have it,
or, to be exact, he has it, the dear departed
slack in his box like a present that,
once the tissue petals were unfolded,
wasn't wanted, like handmade socks
in some unspeakable plaid. Well,
that's okay, just shove this box over
and go on to the next, which might be,
at last, Malibu Barbie or electric
trains. We are gathered to celebrate,
even if the givers got it wrong again –
you think it's going to be a new house,
and it is, a sort of sub-basement
sub-efficiency and they've given you
fee simple absolute, a form of forever
the law calls a *freehold,* though you
paid with your life. And we others
got the flowers and our fancy clothes,
a smoky set from a wind instrument,
food and decent wines whose outer wraps
guarantee there'll be no disappointment.
Of course, we had to buy the wine
ourselves – but that's our work, from
picking the grape to gluing the label,
and in time (which is not the opposite of,
but instead comes before, *out of time*)

we learn to take it up gladly.
Hell, let's celebrate that too, even
toast the givers, because they once
gave us you, and ourselves, gifts so good
we were willing to pay in blood,
as after all we will, when the piper's final note
comes in its windowed envelope that lets us
see inside and glimpse the bill.

Suite: Riverside, Iowa (Stumptown)

i

Some Kind of Prayer

Who didn't love promises at six,
the skyfallen grace of language made flesh
in front of our dazzled, developing eyes,
staggering to us as a new calf might.
We bent our own scabby knees to greet it:
word for word what would be so,
would be so, not the rote tease
of scripture but what is swallowed,
breathed, said in the body.

What I believe about sacraments
is they happen not under glass,
witnessed and sung to, but maybe alongside
a barbed fence on a prickly afternoon
when a Poland China sow takes it into her mind
to memorize the smell of you.

Who will climb out of his story
to save my life? The redwing blackbird
compresses himself to bring out sound,
so much music per ounce, his tail
bearing down hard while his red flash
widens as if he were flying.
We call it song, tuneless,
explicit: this is my river reed,
my reed. Some things may not be

legends after all – the dolphin's
chameleon death, the opossum
penis bones oldtime hunters brag over.
Don't we want our hunters a little
less vulgar? Their shirts cleaner?
Or shall we serve them supper as they are
and sweep up the mud later?

Whistle what you like, you never really
know what you're saying to birds.

ii

So Far

I thought from the leaf's integrity
a visible language would sprout.
Something green, to make it easier.

I go wading because I need to.
In the intertidal waters
to put your foot down
is to feel an erasure of land.
The ghost crabs climb up,
blue clawed, watching with tall eyes.

"Pick one," he said,
and sighted on the Dragon's head.
He launched a whole clip,
supersonic, one in five a tracer,
a fire scar. No star fell,
wing-shot, burning down.

Somewhere inside history
the trustfulness slipped out.
Now I want the luck of seeing
the orioles' fledglings
climbing out of the nest at Stumptown,
afloat on open air.

iii

After Midnight

The stars as if the moon were crushed,
electric wires knifing a noise into the dark.
I came to practice not being terrified
on this name- and number-less gravel road.
The constellations almost call out for recognition
and me with no map, no compass. The dust the car
kicked up all but settled, stars down to the horizon.
In the city there's only a smudgy reddened sunfall
into a nightlong glow of chemicals and lamplight,
but here the sky throws its net down from every
direction to pull me drowning out of my sea.

iv

The Change I Was Afraid of & Wanted

In the presence of heavy corn, taller
by now than I am, and owls hooting
in the trees, and a wild turkey cry,
my fingers have opened to show me
an empty palm. The old woman,
restless in her blindness, told me
I'd see the face of my enemy
right in my hand someday. And then
my mystic savior would come and
pierce me through with the blinding light.
I was ten. I believed her. I began
to watch for an enemy's stare from
inside my body. Some nights I felt
demons jostling, reaching for my hand.
My left hand, in which another woman
found two marriages and an ocean.
This year, I've married myself to
corn and animals who know I am not
the wilderness. I never stopped hungering
for the angel's approach, though I could
never think of mysticism without
feeling foolish. Who knew that corn
flies above its own dark wings?
My enemy's face has been plain
on my palm all these years, and his
empty name was easy on my lips because
I am blind and not blind even now.

v

Closer

Most of what matters to me
can be touched, but must be left
untouched, the bell hunched
over its silence until the moment
of telling. St. Augustine said
when he prayed, even the straw
beneath his knees shouted to
distract him. Today is the day
of the small-eared rabbit lying
on her side, at ease near me.
I don't believe animals can tell
who they don't need to be afraid of,
though if I had that gift, I would have
tipped myself like brimmed-over wine
into his arms anyway. The ducks
in front of me now sway in their
onelegged sleep like dreaming trees.
What would it feel like to stroke
a mallard's purple wingflash?
Every moment in this dulling light
at the edge of a lake brings
a harvest of desires. What tames
these ducks? Occasional food,
but they came back to me a second time
after not receiving food. Not
trust, not stupidity, but a habit
of patience and a long wanting.

Notes

Limbo, That Abolished World Limbo was the abode of unbaptized souls and of souls of the just who died before Christ. The Roman Catholic church deleted Limbo from its doctrine in 2007, saying that Limbo represented an unduly strict interpretation of salvation.

Survival of the Good Enough Darwin developed the theory of natural selection based in part on his researches into the beaks of Galapagos finches. He found that the birds' beaks were specially adapted to unique foods on their separate islands. Darwin's finch collection is still preserved in the British Museum.

Apple Traditionally, Eve is supposed to have tempted Adam with an apple. A variant tradition is that the fruit of Man's downfall was a pomegranate.

Friday The "oriented" reference is to the questions medics ask people with head trauma: typically, if they know the date, where they are, and who is President.

But Never A Smile Without A Cat The reference is to *Alice in Wonderland*. When the Cheshire Cat lingeringly disappears, Alice remarks that she has seen "a cat without a smile, but never a smile without a cat."

Everything AND the Circus e.e. cummings once remarked "Damn everything but the circus." I use it ironically, as I hope you can tell from the poem. When it came to Washington, DC, the Ringling Bros & Barnum and Bailey Circus used to (and may still) parade its animals up Third Street NW to its fairgrounds. They went right past the Labor Department at Third and Constitution, where my office window overlooked the spectacle.

On The Way In This Morning   The confused composer was Meyerbeer, who, because of Chopin's unique way of playing, mistook a piece in common time for waltz time.

"…Posing as a Somdomite"   The phrase comes from a note the Marquis of Queensbury (he of the gentlemanly rules of boxing) left for Oscar Wilde at Wilde's club. It was the opening salvo of a war, waged in the courts, between these two men which ended in Wilde being ruined and forced to leave England. Bosie was the Marquis's son, with whom Wilde had an affair. The misspelling is Queensbury's, but I couldn't bring myself to put "sic" in a poem's title.

Chopin at Nohant   Nohant was George Sand's country home, where Chopin lived with her for part of the time they spent together. Solange was Sand's daughter; when Solange was an adult, Chopin took her side against her mother in a bitter quarrel.

That Photo of Jack & Jerry   The photo is of the poets Jack Gilbert and Gerald Stern and is on the cover of Jerry's book *The Red Coal*. They both grew up in what Jerry called "medieval Pittsburgh" and were life-long friends. The photo shows them young and brimming with energy and joy in Paris. This is my fancy based on the photo and is not necessarily in accord with actual facts. For example, Jack Gilbert denied ever drinking the worst wine gladly.

Lifework   This poem is for William Matthews, in memoriam.

Suite: Riverside, Iowa (Stumptown)   Stumptown is a local name for Riverside, Iowa: a hamlet, or a village (anyway, a very small place). Near it lies the confluence of the Iowa and English rivers, a really good birdwatching site. In *Star Trek* lore, Riverside is the hometown of Captain James C. Kirk, and in the years that I went there, there was a sign saying "Vulcan Embassy" in one of the vacant storefronts.

Acknowledgements

Ploughshares: "Poplar Pond, November," "The Same Apple Twice," "Limbo, That Abolished World," "Cezanne"

The Atlantic: "Closer"

Innisfree: "First Love," "A House of Three Animals"

Alaska Quarterly: "Lifework"

Legal Studies Forum: "Of All Earthly Things," "Apple," "Wishbone," "Liam," "Third Snow in a Week," "Vieux Port," "August," "St. Praxeda Sopping Up Blood," "Hymn to Apollo," "The Change I Was Afraid of & Wanted," "Mourning, Saturday," "A Dish Best Eaten Cold," "Darkness Travels at the Speed of Light," "Old Flames," "Save Time"

About the Author

Laura Fargas was born in Berkeley and was educated at the University of California, Berkeley, the University of Pennsylvania Law School, and the Iowa Writers Workshop. For 27 years, she worked for the federal government, specializing in occupational safety and health litigation. Her previous publications include *Reflecting What Light We Can't Absorb* (Riverstone Press 1993) and *An Animal of the Sixth Day* (Texas Tech University Press 1996).

www.ingramcontent.com/pod-product-compliance
Lightning Source LLC
Chambersburg PA
CBHW021023090426
42738CB00007B/879